How to Catch a Keeper!

by Stephanie Mulligan

Illustrated by Connie Rand

McSea Books

To my husband, Matthew –
You are the perfect husband and the best father.

To Clara, Emmett, & Lena –
You will forever bring immeasurable joy and purpose to my life.

SM

To my husband, Lee, who loves me with all his heart, and lets my creative spirit flourish.

CR

"And he saith unto them,
Follow me, and I will make you fishers of men."

Matthew 4:19

Manufactured by Regent Publishing Services Ltd Printed October 2021 in ShenZhen, China

Hardcover ISBN: 978-1-7323020-5-1
Library of Congress Control Number: 2018905983

www.McSeaBooks.com

Publisher's Cataloging-in-Publication Data
provided by Five Rainbows Cataloging Services

Names: Mulligan, Stephanie, author. | Rand, Connie, illustrator.
Title: How to catch a keeper! / Stephanie Mulligan ; Connie Rand, illustrator.
Description: Lincoln, ME : McSea Books, 2020.
Identifiers: LCCN 2018905983 (print) | ISBN 978-1-7323020-0-6 (softcover) | ISBN 978-1-7323020-5-1 (hardcover) | Summary: Two children vacationing in Maine with their family learn about lobster fishing. | Audience: K-5.
Subjects: LCSH: Lobster fishers--Maine--Juvenile literature. | Lobster industry--Maine--Juvenile literature. | American lobster fisheries--Maine--Juvenile literature. | Fishing boats--Maine--Juvenile literature. | Picture books for children. | BISAC: JUVENILE NONFICTION / Animals / Marine Life. | JUVENILE NONFICTION / Readers / Beginner.
Classification: LCC SH380.25.A45 H69 2020 (print) | LCC SH380.25.A45 (ebook) | DDC 338.3/72538409741--dc23.

How to Catch a Keeper!

Luke and Layla's summer
has finally begun,
and a trip to the Maine Coast
is sounding really fun!

Out the door they go
into the early dawn.
Their dad points to the map
and begins to ramble on –

"Summer by the coast
is *always* full of fun!
Let's get moving right away,
and go enjoy the sun!

There are many ways to play in Maine
you're sure to really like.
I know of fun spots to explore
and islands we can bike!

There are cruises and museums,
and lighthouses galore,
but I think my favorite
is the Lucky Catch Tour!"

"What's so great about *this* tour?"
Luke and Layla say.

Dad says,
"We'll get to ride a lobster boat
on this very day!

There's so much to learn
about lobstering, dears.

When Captain Tom speaks,
please perk up your ears!"

"This is a hands-on tour,"
Tom tells everyone.
*"Rain or shine,
we'll always have fun!*

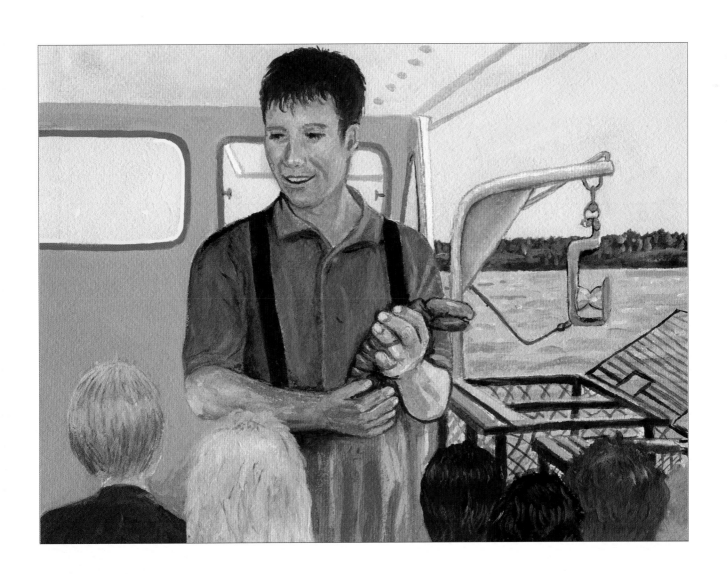

You'll need aprons and gloves
to protect you from mud.
The traps sometimes splash
when they land with a thud."

On the big, red mat
Captain Tom stands,
where the winch pulls up traps
and could injure your hands.

There's his sweet dog Sammy
with black and white hair.
She listens so well
that she's allowed to stand there.

It's easy to see
that she loves Casco Bay.

How excited she gets
spotting buoys all day!

The buoys with red tops
and green stripes around —
these all mark the spots
where Tom's traps are found.

Tom says to the crowd,

"Step up, if you're daring!
It's time to fill the bait bags
with salty, smelly herring."

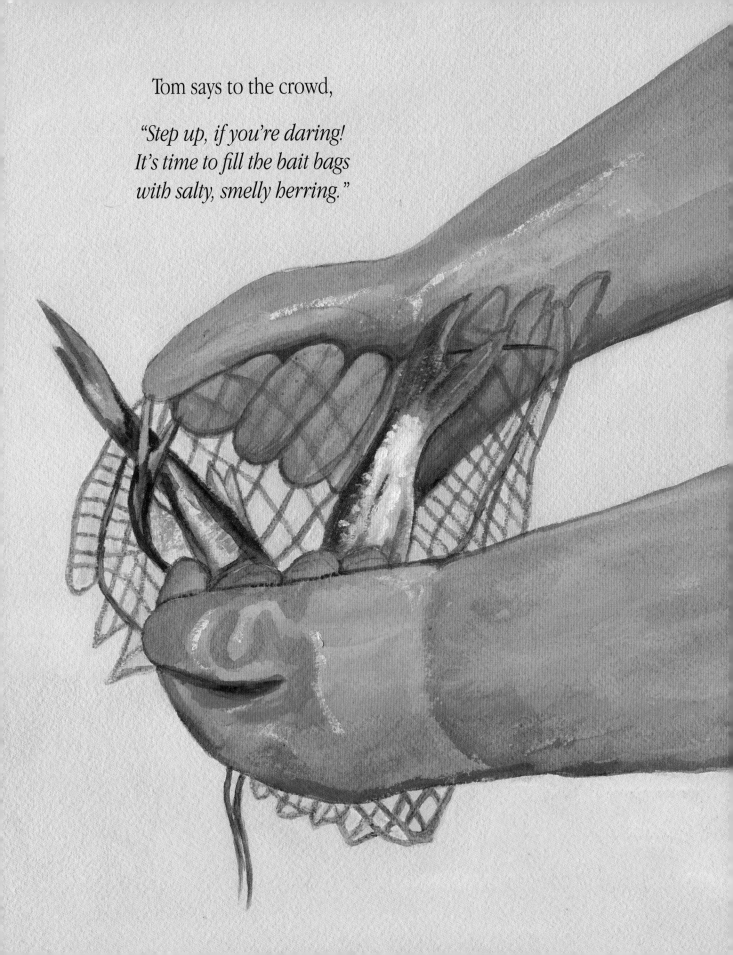

Layla spies a buoy;
it's the right one to snag!

Captain Tom grabs his gaff
and the winch begins to drag.

Tom is first to see the catch –
There's a *lobster* inside to check!

He pulls one from the trap
that's dripping on the deck.

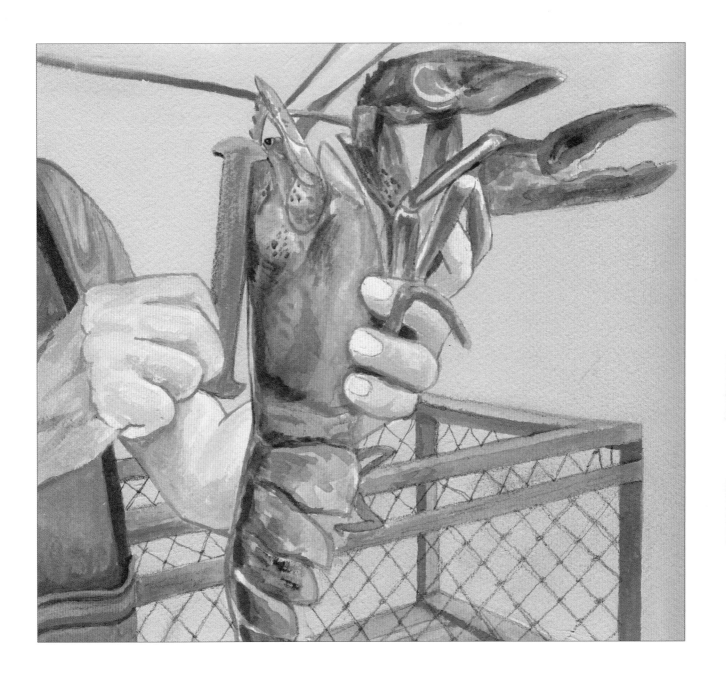

He measures the lobster's carapace,
from its eye to the start of its tail.

Is it the right size to keep?

Is it a female or male?

It's a female with some eggs.
Back in the sea she'll go!
But first he'll notch her tail
to let the next fisherman know!

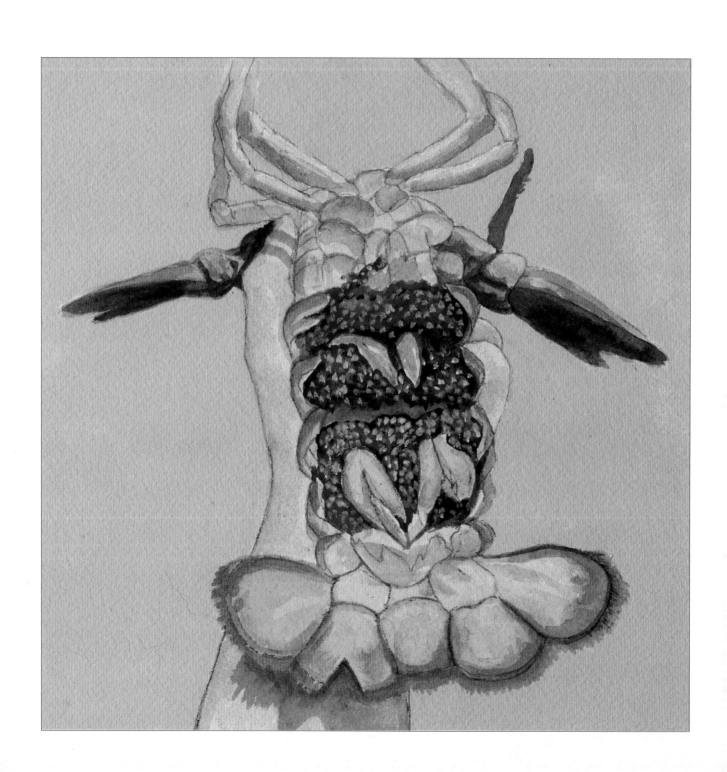

There's other sea life in the trap:
sea stars, crabs, and kelp.
Someone has to send them back;
Luke and Layla help.

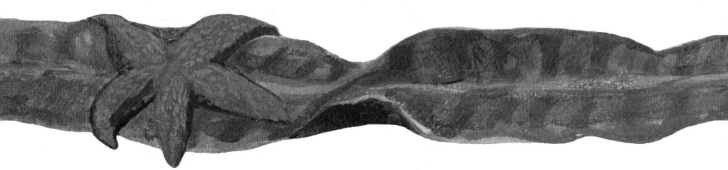

The empty trap now needs new bait,
the old goes off the side.
Hungry seagulls fly above
and somehow don't collide.

The children help to push the trap
back into the sea.

"Hands flat against the trap," Tom says,
"until I count to three."

"We have more traps to prep," says Tom,
"and they'll set for three days at least.
Let's fill those bags again
and hope for a lobster feast!"

Now Tom steers the *Lucky Catch*
over by Seal Rock
where seals rest with cormorants
amongst a seagull flock.

Two more traps . . . another lobster!

"Watch those claws and legs!"

This one is a KEEPER!
It's a female without eggs.

The pincer and crusher claws
will certainly need bands.
The kids can use the banding tool,
even with small hands!

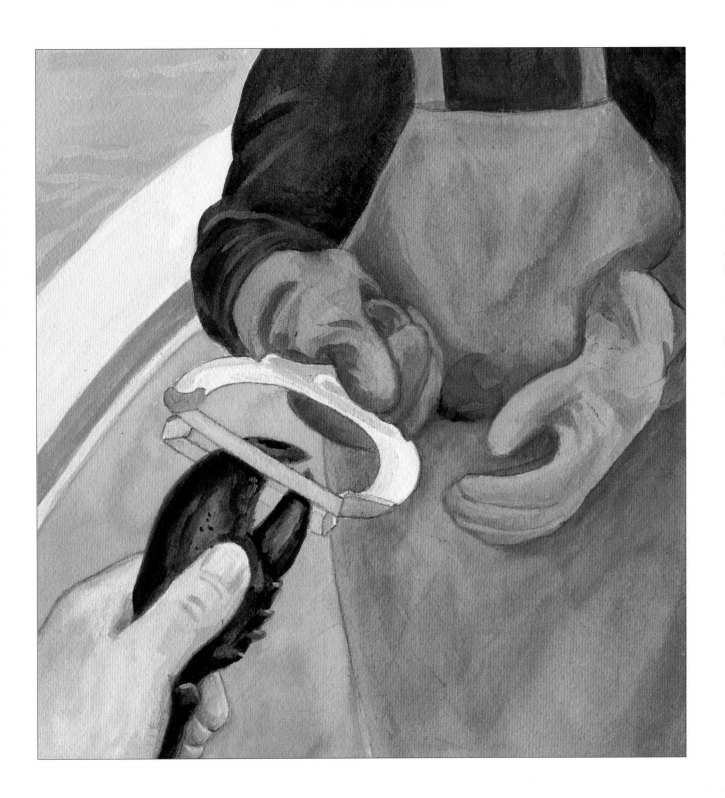

Here's Luke with the keeper —
it's a good-sized one!
He poses for a photo and says,
"This was *really* fun!"

Tom drives the boat back in.
A crew member gathers the gear.
The kids run up the ramp and say,

"Let's come back next year!"

Lobstering Lingo

Banding tool: A tool designed to help put rubber bands around lobster claws. To use it, place a thick rubber band at the tip of the tool and squeeze the handle on the other end. This process opens up the rubber band so you can safely secure it onto the claw.

Buoy (boo-ee): An anchored float that lobstermen attach to their line or rope to help them find their traps.

Carapace (care-a-pace): The upper section of a lobster's shell that covers its body. This part of the lobster must be measured to see if it is within the legal size to keep.

Casco Bay: A small body of water that opens into the Gulf of Maine. The Gulf of Maine is part of the Atlantic Ocean and is located on the east coast of North America.

Cormorant: A large, black bird found along the coast of Maine. The double-crested cormorant can be seen hanging out on the rocks and ledges of Casco Bay, where it dries out its wings.

Gaff: A tool used by lobstermen to grab a buoy and pull it up to the winch. A gaff is a stick (an old hockey stick in Captain Tom's case!) with a hook on one end.

Herring (hair-ing): A fish found in the Atlantic Ocean that is a popular choice for bait and is used by many Maine lobstermen.

Keeper: A lobster that is a legal size to keep. Lobstermen in Maine use a double-sided gauge to measure the lobster's carapace. They measure from the very back of the eye socket to the end of the carapace. A keeper must be at least 3.25 inches but no longer than 5 inches. If a lobster's carapace exceeds 5 inches, it falls under the "oversized" category. In Maine, an oversized lobster is thrown back, whether it is female or male.

Kelp: A type of algae that grows in the ocean. Ribbon Kelp is the name of a common kind of seaweed that makes its way into many Maine lobster traps. This name comes from the kelp's wavy, ribbon-like appearance.

 **Notch (also known as "V-notch"):** A mark that lobstermen make on breeding female lobsters. This mark is made using a sharp tool like the back of the measuring gauge. They cut a small notch in the shape of a "v" on the second tail-flipper from the right. The notch tells other lobstermen that she produces eggs and must be released back to the ocean. Not every female lobster is a breeder, so notching her tail is important because hopefully she'll grow larger and keep hatching more lobsters that you can catch!

 Pincer & Crusher Claws: The two front claws on a lobster. The pincer claw is the smaller one. A lobster uses its claws to crush and shred its food.

 Sea Stars: A marine animal also known as a starfish.

 Winch: A device that lobstermen use to pull their lobster traps up to the boat. Lobstermen will wrap their rope around the winch in order to keep the rope untangled and to save them time hauling their traps.

About the Author

Stephanie Mulligan worked on the *Lucky Catch*, a lobster fishing tour boat, with Captain Tom Martin for eight summers. She wanted to capture the experience and remember it forever because each time she stepped on the boat was a new journey, and it never got old! After growing up in Otisfield, a beautiful village in western Maine, working for Captain Tom gave her the opportunity to meet people from all over the world who wanted to learn about lobstering! This was the perfect summer job combining the best of both worlds — education and the Maine outdoors.

She graduated from the University of Maine at Orono with her B.S. in Elementary Education and a concentration in English. Then she began writing her first book to illustrate these wonderful lobster excursions.

Stephanie lives in Maine with her husband and their darling children.

© Photo by Keith Nuki

About the Illustrator

Connie Rand, a native of Lincoln, Maine, graduated in 1969 from Portland School of Fine and Applied Art, now Maine College of Art, in Portland, from which she received an honorary Bachelor of Fine Arts in 2000. Her drawings and paintings are owned by collectors all over the United States and Canada. Connie illustrates *Quilter's World* magazine and other quilting publications for Annie's Publishing in Berne, Indiana. She and her husband Lee own Rand Advertising in Lincoln. They also own and maintain www.WelcomeToLincolnMaine.com, a website showcasing the Lincoln area, where they live with their three cats Ebenezer Scrooge, Marley, and Tiny Tim. To find out more visit connierand.com.

© Photo by Lee Rand

© Photo by Keith Nuki

About the Captain

Captain Tom Martin began lobstering as a summer job working for his neighbor. He has been a licensed commercial lobster fisherman since 1985. During the summer of 1996, he began sharing the real Maine lobstering experience with passengers aboard his boat, *Lucky Catch*.

Captain Tom and his crew provide an educational and unforgettable adventure on each tour. Whether you're interested in the history of Casco Bay, learning about Maine's economy and conservation laws, or soaking up the scenery during a private charter — look no further! The Captain and his crew are waiting for you!

To find out more information on how to make your vacation in Maine even more memorable, contact Captain Tom or a *Lucky Catch* crew member:

(207) 761-0941
info@luckycatch.com
www.luckycatch.com

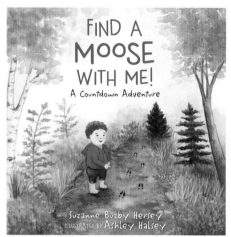
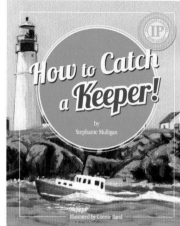
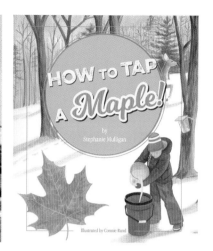